Start Online Freelancing Today

A Beginner's Guide to Working From Home

A PawPrint Life Upgrades Book

© **Copyright 2020 PawPrint Digital Publishing - All rights reserved.**

The content contained within this book may not be reproduced, duplicated or transmitted without direct written permission from the author or the publisher.

Under no circumstances will any blame or legal responsibility be held against the publisher, or author, for any damages, reparation, or monetary loss due to the information contained within this book, either directly or indirectly.

Legal Notice:

This book is copyright protected. It is only for personal use. You cannot amend, distribute, sell, use, quote or paraphrase any part, or the content within this book, without the consent of the author or publisher.

Disclaimer Notice:

Please note the information contained within this document is for educational and entertainment purposes only. All effort has been executed to present accurate, up to date, reliable, complete information. No warranties of any kind are declared or implied. Readers acknowledge that the author is not engaging in the rendering of legal, financial, medical or professional advice. The content within this book has been derived from various sources. Please consult a licensed professional before attempting any techniques outlined in this book.

By reading this document, the reader agrees that under no circumstances is the author responsible for any losses, direct or indirect, that are incurred as a result of the use of information contained within this document, including, but not limited to, errors, omissions, or inaccuracies.

PawPrint Life Upgrades

The PawPrint Life Upgrades series is a series of books commissioned by PawPrint Digital Publishing to help people improve their mental and physical wellbeing, strive for personal success, and realize their life goals.

Table of Contents

Introduction...1
Chapter One: Assessing Your Skills...................................5
   Getting Started...6
   Writer and Editor..7
   Graphic Designer and Programmer..........................8
   Marketer..10
   Photographer..12
   Accountant and Bookkeeper...................................13
   Recruiter...14
   Salesperson...15
   Customer Service Representative...........................16
   Blockchain Expert...17
   Teacher...17
   Virtual Assistant...19
   Other Professions...20
Chapter Two: All-Round Freelance Services....................22
   Upwork...24
   Fiverr..29
   Freelancer...33
   Summary...38
Chapter Three: Programming and Graphic Design...........40
   Programming..40
   Toptal..40
   Gigster..43
   Gun.io...45
   Graphic Design...47
   99Designs...48
   Crowdspring...50
   Summary...51
Chapter Four: Writing and Editing...................................53
   Copyscape...54
   iWriter..55
   Guru..57
   PeoplePerHour...58

    Constant Content..60
    Summary...61
Chapter Five: Marketing...62
    ClearVoice...64
    OnSite..65
    LinkedIn..67
    Contently...68
Conclusion...71
Online Resources..73

Introduction

A typical corporate job, office politics, and fixed working hours are not everybody's cup of tea. Nor is running your own business. If neither of these concepts of earning a living entices you, going freelance can be an interesting approach. Working as a full-time freelancer comes with a lot of perks, personal freedom being on the top of the list. You can work and take leave at your convenience, set your working schedule as per your preference, and work in the comfort of your own home. Moreover, you can save time and money on the commute and won't have to listen to a nagging boss all day. Basically, it is perfect for those who don't want to be confined to an office for a typical nine-to-five job and want to achieve financial stability while enjoying the benefits of flexibility.

The concept of freelancing sounds alluring to many. However, this career path comes with its own challenges. First, you must find clients in your niche who are open to working with freelancers. Second, you always need to make sure you have enough assignments to meet your income targets. It doesn't end there. There are certain contractual nuances and formalities to sort out, prices to negotiate, and payment arrangements to make.

All this must sound comforting and intimidating at the same time. In order to make a decision, you'll need a few answers to questions like:

- Where do I begin working as a freelancer?
- What is the earning potential? How much can I get paid?
- What kind of skills are in demand?
- How reliable can this profession be?
- How can I ensure continuity and progression?

Typically, setting out to be a freelancer seems rosier on paper than it actually is, but it doesn't have to be this way. Thanks to the mighty Internet, there is an answer to everything. There are several online platforms that bring together free-

Introduction

lancers with varied skill sets and employers from around the globe. Most of their users are well-organized, transparent, meticulous, and mindful of legal details in contracts. Not only are these websites and platforms easy to use, but they also help you earn a steady income and build a strong network with like-minded people of various nationalities.

As for skills, whether you are a writer, editor, designer, illustrator, blogger, teacher, programmer, consultant—or if you practice pretty much any other profession—you can always find a client who is seeking relevant skills for related projects. You will be at an advantage if you possess more than one skill and can combine them to find projects. And with the onset of these freelance services, clients across the world have become highly dependent on freelancers to get work done, instead of hiring full-time employees. This can help you find more work on a daily basis and you can polish your skills along the way.

Throughout the chapters ahead, we will discuss the general freelance services that are most popular among the majority of freelancers, digging into specific skills, and targeting freelance platforms that adhere to these skills. Since information on this subject is somewhat scattered, it can be difficult to get answers quickly. This is where this book will help you.

Not only will it help you to determine the skill that you want to work on and polish, but it will also guide you through all possible freelance services that you can target to make a steady income. Read on and get inspired to begin your full-time freelancing career today.

Chapter One: Assessing Your Skills

Your credibility as a freelancer depends on your quality of work, punctuality, and the way you handle your clients. Your work is a major part of your identity, and its fate will depend on your success as a freelancer. This is directly proportional to the portfolio you build and the skills you possess. A lot of freelancing services encourage clients and freelancers to do business through their platforms and benefit from it in numerous ways. Clients can get professional work done without going over budget, and freelancers can benefit from lucrative paychecks while polishing their skills.

If you think that your primary skill isn't exactly aligned with a freelancing discipline, you are wrong. With the increasing demand in almost every discipline across the world, people are searching for more freelancers in every niche. And with freelancing no longer being a euphemism for a low-paying job, you can definitely find gigs and earn a comfortable living, regardless of the skills you possess.

Getting Started

Take out a piece of paper or open a note on your phone or computer. Start by writing down the professional skills you know you already have. Next, think of projects that you have done in the past that you enjoyed. Think of the skills that were involved in bringing those projects to life. Write these down as well, even if they don't seem relevant. You will be surprised what you'll find once you start browsing the available work on freelancing websites. We will take a look at this list again in the next chapter.

The following is a list of common in-demand freelancers. Have a look and see if you have the skills to undertake them. If you don't have the skills now, but are interested in one of these careers, look at sites like Udemy, Thinkific, Teachable, Coursera, and SkillShare to see what is available to get those skills.

Writer and Editor

With thousands of new websites and blogs emerging on a daily basis, the demand for writers and editors has increased. If you possess the basic skill of writing content or editing written work, why not turn it into a full-time job? A lot of people are getting into self-publishing and are on the constant lookout for content writers, editors, and proofreaders. Depending on the quality of your work, you can make up to $40 an hour.

Even if you are not an expert in a topic you end up working on, you can always research and fetch information to produce content. And if you possess specific skills as a writer, you can target clients that are looking for copywriters, fiction writers, as well as writers for web content, instructional manuals, and even e-books. Since the demand is skyrocketing, it is highly unlikely that you will run out of assignments for a while. Writing is no longer considered a recreational activity for creative hermits. You can make as much money out of it as you would with a typical full-time job.

There are a number of freelance platforms—such as Upwork, Freelancer, Fiverr, and many others—where you can sign up and benefit from the postings on a daily basis. We'll take a closer look at them in the upcoming chapters.

Graphic Designer and Programmer

Whether it is a small-scale startup or a high-scale business, clients are looking for designers and programmers depending on their project requirements. The demand for graphic and web designers is increasing, and it is further estimated to grow up to 61% in the coming years. The companies are benefited by getting work that is edgy and fresh while keeping their budgets aligned. Also, not many companies hire full-time graphic designers and heavily rely on freelancers to get full-time work done. The most basic skill that a designer must possess is the knowledge of design

Chapter One: Assessing Your Skills

software such as Photoshop and Illustrator. Depending on your level of work and experience, you can easily make $20 to $150 an hour.

Not just graphic designers, but the demand for web designers and developers is also high. Every company today realizes the importance of having a website. It is slowly becoming more of a necessity. Web designers are responsible for determining a wide range of factors, from the interface to the aesthetic layout. Since websites create the first impression on almost every client, it is necessary for all companies to build a professional-looking site. If you are an expert in web design and development, this is your chance.

Programming and software development are other popular niches that carry an unbelievable earning potential. Software and mobile app development is a particularly tough skill to master, which is why companies hire freelance programmers that have impressive skills, and they are ready to pay what is demanded. A lot of professional coders and programmers quit their jobs in high-scale multinational companies these days, just to work as freelancers and make more money. This shows the earning potential of a freelance programmer.

Marketer

Content and social media marketing ranks in the top tiers of the most in-demand skills as a freelancer. Every kind and scale of business requires a proficient marketer to build their brand and generate public awareness. And since clients are realizing this need for a marketer, they are hiring freelancers who can stand out among the other marketing agencies and provide out-of-the-box strategies. Among the various marketing channels, social media marketing and content marketing are the top sub-niches. Since billions of people are using social media today, social media marketing is necessary to make users aware of brands. You can earn a hefty income working as a freelance marketer—given that you have an impeccable profile and portfolio—because the ma-

Chapter One: Assessing Your Skills

jority of clients have accepted this move as a necessary expense by now.

If you think that you've always been interested in marketing but couldn't quite get a grasp of it, you should consider enrolling in a certificate course or training. Apart from this, you can acquire a few more skills such as email marketing and SEO to form a complete digital marketing package. This will strengthen your resume and increase your chances of getting hired.

These three skills are in high demand today. If you are planning to take a course or brush up on your skills, you should definitely seek one of these, unless you are uninterested or looking for another niche. In the following chapters, you will learn about the top freelance services and platforms dedicated to these three skills and how you can benefit from them. Check out the rest of the list to pick a skill that aligns with specific industries or particular requirements of clients in this gig economy.

Photographer

Do you have a passion for photography? Are you constantly praised for your photography skills? Do you own a camera? If yes, you should definitely consider working as a freelance photographer. A lot of companies and people are looking for photographers to shoot events such as weddings, birthday parties, or professional gatherings. A few startups and bloggers also hire freelance photographers for photoshoots through which they brand their products or services. You can also sign up for stock websites to sell photographs and earn from respective clauses or per download of your image. To enhance your profile, you will need to build a strong portfolio that covers the type of photography you are proficient in.

Even though there has been a sharp decline in the demand for photographers in traditional media, you can still grab projects that are based on portrait or commercial photography. The key is to stand out. Yes, there is a lot of competition in the discipline of photography, but you can still fetch

Chapter One: Assessing Your Skills

projects if your work is impressive. If you think you have what it takes but just are not ready yet, you can brush up on your skills, experiment, and build your portfolio in the meantime. You can also complete a few assignments for free to strengthen your profile.

Accountant and Bookkeeper

You might be surprised to see this category as an in-demand freelance skill. But you must know that a lot of companies are looking for freelance accountants and bookkeepers as we speak. A lot of startups do not have a large enough budget to hire a full-time accountant, which is why they rely on freelancers who are competent accountants. To work as one, you need to possess relevant skills and have knowledge about all the top accounting software that is currently flooding the market. Depending on your level of experience, you can easily make a proper living out of this.

Working as a freelance accountant would require you to look after financial accounts and statements from home. Even though there are several useful software products available today, every company still requires the help of a human brain one way or another. For instance, tax deductions are difficult to comprehend, and that is why the demand for a working professional will always remain high. Hiring a freelance bookkeeper also allows the company to focus on other important tasks and daily activities, which will help with the growth of the company.

Recruiter

Being a recruiter is no longer an 'office-going' job. A lot of recruiting professionals are taking to freelancing and working from the comfort of their homes. Many companies are also hiring freelance recruiters to search for competent employees across various sectors, with IT, medicine, and engineering leading the charts. At times, freelance recruiters are also given the responsibility of interviewing and shortlisting candidates for the company, which saves a lot of time and gives the

Chapter One: Assessing Your Skills

company the chance to hire proficient employees. To find work as a freelance recruiter, your experience and expertise would be of the utmost importance.

Salesperson

This is another surprising sector that is actually doing well in the freelancers' niche. Companies are hiring freelance sales representatives that are often independent and experienced. Not only is it cost-effective for companies, but it is also more efficient and advantageous when it comes to driving sales. Small-scale startups are investing in freelance sales representatives mainly due to their budget confinement, but the results seem to be effective. This has led to the success of freelancers in this discipline. Individual sales representatives usually have more contacts and a wider network, and they can easily convince the parties to buy relevant products and services. If you have been working as a sales representative in a company, try working as a freelancer for a while to test the waters. It will give you a chance to expand your network and probably earn more money than you used to.

Customer Service Representative

Working as a customer service representative is one of the most convenient jobs you can take up as a freelancer. This is because you will simply have to talk to customers on the phone or probably online. For this, you will require intangible skills such as ease of communication, quick decision-making, and negotiation. Even if you have another job or a skill set you're putting to good use, you can simply take this up as a part-time job to add to your monthly earnings. Since the job usually requires you to work after-hours, it could be great to earn a few extra bucks and make your spare time more productive. It fairly aligns with moonlighting, which is why it ranks among the top skills to have as a freelancer.

Chapter One: Assessing Your Skills

Blockchain Expert

The blockchain ecosystem is currently in high demand and will probably continue to be so in the coming years. It was actually meant for cryptocurrency but is now excessively used for the development of a number of industries, which includes insurance, law, healthcare, and governance. In basic terms, blockchain is keeping a record of bitcoin or cryptocurrency transactions, which are inherently changing the current face of technology. A lot of big companies such as Samsung and IBM have already leveraged blockchain, and others are likely to follow suit.

Since there are not as many blockchain experts to level the demand today, you should grab this opportunity to garner more projects and build your skills. You can find numerous online blockchain courses and certifications hosted by professionals to learn more about this discipline.

Teacher

A freelance teacher might sound odd, but this

concept is actually trending. Moreover, teaching is one of the most in-demand skills that companies are looking for. "But how does freelance teaching or tutoring work," you might ask. For this, you need to work as an online teacher. A lot of students prefer learning online as these courses are more convenient and accessible from all around the world, which is why the demand for online tutoring has gone up.

If you are an expert in specific subjects such as business, you can become an online coach, too. These subjects are highly sought-after, and you can easily find prospective students who are looking for proven business strategies, tips, and ideas to start their businesses. Again, this is another successful freelancing venture that you can engage in after your official working hours and even during your retirement. There has recently been a sharp increase in the demand for business and career coaches. A lot of people are tired of their jobs and looking to change careers. They need professional advice and assurance in doing so, which is

Chapter One: Assessing Your Skills

why they seek the help of career coaches. You, as a freelance career coach, can offer information and guidance on interviews, job searches, resumes, and self-confidence.

If you have the necessary teaching skills and experience, you can take up online teaching. All you need is a serene setting, a working laptop, high-speed Internet, and a quiet space in your home. You can browse sites like Tutor and BuddySchool, sign up to start working, and make some extra money during your free hours.

Virtual Assistant

The main benefit of working as a virtual assistant is that you don't need a certification or a formal education to do this. If you are new to freelancing and are looking for a skill, you could consider working as a virtual assistant. A VA is responsible for handling administrative tasks such as setting appointments, keeping track of the logistics, handling important emails, or keeping a record of important events. As the name suggests, this is a 'virtual' position, which means you'll work from the comfort of your own home while staying connected through the Internet, even if you're miles away or halfway across the world.

Another major benefit of being a virtual assistant is that a huge number of industries and clients are looking for this skill. Whether it is an entrepreneur, a doctor, a coach, or an author, people around the world are becoming aware of the importance of an assistant; more importantly, the perks of hiring a virtual one. There has been a rapid increase in the number of freelancers working as virtual assistants on a full-time basis. This is why your chances of finding work are high in this niche. Still, to boost your chances in this competitive field, you can consider investing in a course or training.

Other Professions

Other professionals that are in high demand in the freelancing world include illustrators or comic artists, babysitters, translators, audio transcrip-

Chapter One: Assessing Your Skills

tionists, bloggers, data entry operators, and video editors. This list will definitely encourage you to figure out and assess your skill set and help you make a wise decision. A lot of these skills have great earning potential, even more than a full-time job at times. Depending on your skill set, proficiency, level of expertise, and years of experience, you can make $100 to $1,000 per hour, which is equivalent to or more than a high-profile job. Sounds intriguing, doesn't it?

Chapter Two: All-Round Freelance Services

This chapter will highlight the topic of all-round freelance services that are targeted to freelancers looking for various projects. It is also for those who have already decided on the skill and service they want to work with and are looking for details regarding specific freelancing platforms.

The entire transaction—from finding a relevant opportunity to pitching your services, from negotiating prices to finalizing the features of assignments, to receiving payment and asking for referrals—is integrated into one single platform. These are highly reliable and can help you find projects of varying skills.

Such platforms make life easier for both freelancers and employers seeking their services. So, if you are a freelancer, you should make sure your skills are marketable on the Internet and get ready to exhibit them to clients from across the globe. This chapter will introduce you to some re-

Chapter Two: All-Round Freelance Services

liable freelancing services that are preferred by the majority of freelancers all around the world. You will also learn how to use these platforms, including the processes of signing up, getting projects, setting your price, making your bids, getting paid, and receiving reviews on your work.

If you are looking to match the skills you wrote down in the previous chapter, sign up to one or more of these general sites and do a search under "Find Work". Depending on the service, you may see skill tags when you click through on a job listing. Take a look at these skills and see if they are things that are in your skill-set. The unfortunate reality is that we tend to discount our own abilities. There are tasks that we have done in the past, sometimes on a routine basis, which we simply don't think of when we are put on the spot. Browsing the project listings can help bring these "unimportant" skills to mind. When you find such a skill, add it to your profile.

Let's take a brief look at three of the most popular and reliable freelancing platforms and how to take maximum advantage of them.

Upwork

Upwork is easily the most popular freelancing platform out there. It is a result of a merger between two popular entities, Elance and oDesk. Upwork claims to have over 12 million registered freelancers and over 5 million clients. The platform posts 3 million jobs annually and facilitates $1 billion worth of work a year. Those are some impressive numbers. Upwork covers a wide range of domains such as web design, writing, graphic design and other creative professions, sales and marketing, data science and analytics, admin support, call center, engineering, architecture, etc. Basically, this platform is leading the market and offering all freelancers a myriad of options to choose from. A handy feature of their front page is that they list the thirty-two top skills and thirty-two trending skills for freelancers. If you click through on one of the skills, it will list the top freelancers on the site with their skill tags listed

Chapter Two: All-Round Freelance Services

below. Take a look at these skills as see which ones appeal to you. It is worth looking at this, even if you will not be signing up with Upwork.

So, how to get started?

Signing Up

Signing up on Upwork is a fairly easy process. You can either log in with your Google account or set up your own Upwork account using your email ID. Make sure you build a complete and comprehensive profile because that will represent your resume and portfolio. Currently, there are millions of registered users, which means that the competition is intense for every job opportunity posted. That is how a detailed profile would help you stand out from the rest. While you are building your profile, it is important to be honest about your skill set and experience. If you land an assignment based on dishonesty and you fail to deliver an acceptable project, your account could be put on hold or even terminated.

The sign-up process will involve uploading a

headshot photo and filling in background details (professional and academic qualifications) along with adding links to your previous work samples or portfolios. You can also select the nature and location of your work, preferred rates, etc. Upwork will take up to 24 hours to verify your credentials and approve your account or reject your application.

Searching for Assignments / Projects

You can find job proposals using the website's search tool, shortlist opportunities that are relevant, and match your price expectation. The next step is to submit a job proposal to the client using the website's internal token called 'Connects.' A free Upwork profile offers 60 Connects per month, so use them judiciously.

The job proposal should include an introductory letter, relevant previous work samples, and answers to the questions the client has asked as a part of the job posting. It goes without saying that the job proposal should be read carefully to en-

Chapter Two: All-Round Freelance Services

sure that you can do justice to the assignment.

If your profile stands out, clients can reach out to you. In this case, you don't need to spend your Connects token.

Setting Your Price

Before you decide on your price, let's talk about Upwork's pricing structure. The platform charges a fee for its services based on the amount you earn from each individual client. For the first $500 earned from an individual client, Upwork charges a 20% service fee. The rate becomes 10% if your earnings from the client range between $500.01 and $10,000, and 5% beyond that point.

Depending on the nature of the work and project, you can either set per-hour pricing or a fixed price for a project. Please note that the prices you decide on will be exclusive of Upwork's fee. If a client approaches you for an assignment and proposes a price, you can negotiate to increase the compensation.

The platform's work diary logs the hourly

project by taking a screenshot randomly every 10 minutes. The fixed-price system is straightforward. You provide the agreed deliverables and get paid the agreed amount.

Making Bids

Given that the platform has millions of users, it is natural that every job posting will have intense competition. So, preparing a bid based on the strength of your portfolio and experience to edge out the competition enhances your chances of being hired. You will get the hang of the price range eventually with a trial-and-error approach.

Getting Paid

Once you fill in relevant tax-related information, you can set up your preferred type of payment option—direct transfers to your local bank account, credit cards, or payment services like PayPal, Payoneer or Skrill. The per-hour projects are billed every week and the payment is processed after you and the client have finished reviewing the work (10 days after the end of the billing period).

Chapter Two: All-Round Freelance Services

In case the project is terminated before completion, Upwork's hourly protection service helps you initiate a dispute process. You can also initiate a dispute process for fixed-rate projects if you are not paid for milestone completion or if the client refuses to pay for a project which, according to you, has been completed.

Rating and Feedback

Upwork has a rating system that is similar to the one used by Uber. The clients rate the freelancers and offer feedback while the freelancers do the same for their employers (on a scale of 5 stars). The ratings help both parties find a suitable partner to achieve their goals.

Fiverr

Fiverr is another popular freelancing platform that has a huge followership and spans across a wide variety of job domains. The platform is a bit informal in the way it is positioned but covers all sorts of professions—even unconventional ones—

including law, design, and music. The jobs/projects are termed 'gigs' and most of them have a starting price of $5, hence the name Fiverr. There are 'gigs' available at much higher values as compared to the other freelancing platforms for assignments that require specific and high-level skills. The platform positions itself as an online service exchange agent, and its popularity among audiences makes it a serious source of income for any freelancer who has a digitally deliverable skill.

Terminology

As we already know, the assignments are termed 'gigs.' If you are a freelancer who is seeking a job, you are called a 'seller.' So, that makes 'buyers' the clients, who can either be companies or individuals. Both buyers and sellers can look for each other based on their requirements.

Signing Up

Again, like Upwork, signing up to be a seller on Fiverr is a straightforward process. You enter

Chapter Two: All-Round Freelance Services

your details and contact information, finish the email confirmation formalities, and you are good to go. The next step is to set up your seller profile, which plays a key role in helping you land a gig. This is, again, a straightforward process where you can make your profile attractive by adding your experience, skill set, and background information. Try to make a good first impression as it will majorly determine your chances of landing assignments.

Once you have set up your seller profile, it is time to create your gig. This section basically contains information regarding your services, requirements, and pricing details. Then, you share the gig (the one you just set up) with potential buyers. Your gig will help the buyers decide if you are the right seller to get the job done.

Sending Offers to Buyers

While setting up a gig would make it easy for buyers to approach you, you can also be proactive and send offers to suitable buyers. You will come across many buyers who describe the type of service they are looking for and post a request for that service. Such requests for services will also include details regarding the expected timeline of task completion, requirements, and the amount they are willing to pay.

There are over 200 work categories on Fiverr and with a proper configuration of your seller profile and gig, you can easily find jobs that suit your skills and earning goals.

Getting Paid

Fiverr takes a 20%fee for the gigs you have completed. Even if you have listed your gig for the minimum amount of $5, there is a scope of upselling it once a potential buyer approaches you. This can be done by adding customizable options to your gig so that buyers can choose them for an additional price. Once the buyer approves your work, the payment is processed and you can receive it through PayPal, prepaid cards, or your bank account.

Chapter Two: All-Round Freelance Services

Feedback and Reviews

Like any other freelancing platform, feedback and reviews are important for both buyers and sellers to thrive in this competitive environment. A high rating will not only make you sought-after by buyers, but it will also rank you higher in searches. A top-quality project submitted in time, good and timely communication, and a friendly approach would definitely increase your ratings.

Moreover, if you complete enough projects with a high rating, you will be promoted from the 'new seller' ranking to a 'top-rated seller' one. Following this, you can avail yourself of a special badge, VIP support, and a place on Fiverr promotions.

Freelancer

The list would be incomplete without Freelancer in it. This platform is a great place for freelancers to meet clients for both online and offline projects. Whether you are a website developer or a babysitter, you can find a job that suits your needs. In many ways, Freelancer is similar to Upwork in terms of operation and structure.

Signing Up

Signing up for Freelancer is free. Like the other two platforms, you sign up with your email ID, verify it, then complete your profile with details such as your name, contact info, country (so that offline projects in your location can be accessed), experience, previous projects, skills, and hourly rate. Also, adding all your skills would open up opportunities for relevant projects. You can bid for a project only if you have at least one relevant skill.

Finding Work

Once you have set up your profile, Freelancer will show you relevant projects based on your skills through the project feed that is located on the top-right corner of your dashboard. The projects can be based on per-hour or fixed-price payments. A unique feature of Freelancer is that you can also find work and get paid by participating in

Chapter Two: All-Round Freelance Services

contests. The contest organizer will post a brief and users can participate by submitting their entries. If your entry is chosen, you win the prize money.

Bidding on Projects

You can use the 'Browse Projects' option to look for relevant projects and click on them to know more. The bidding section can be found below the project description where you can enter your bidding amount. You should also indicate the time you would take to complete the project, compile a detailed and compelling proposal by including your portfolio, split tasks into milestones, and fix prices for each milestone (the total amount should match the project price). Once you are done with these steps, simply press the 'Place Bid' button.

Once it is done, employers may contact you to discuss the details and the scope of the project, and to finalize milestone payments. These conversations can be fulfilled through the platform's native messenger feature. Once the project is awarded, you will get 36 hours to accept it.

Submitting Contest Entry

Browse for a contest you wish to join, read the brief, ask the contest holder for clarifications if necessary, and click on 'Submit My Entry' when you are ready. Add a title to your entry, upload the related file, declare that the content is original, enter your selling price (in case your entry doesn't win but the contest holder still wishes to buy it, this will be the payable price), and click on 'Submit Entry.'

If your entry wins, you and the contest holder will have to sign an 'Intellectual Property Transfer Agreement,' after which your prize money will be transferred to your account.

Getting Paid

Freelancer charges you a fee of 10% of the project price or $5 (whichever is higher). This amount is charged as soon as you accept the project. The charges are fixed as both hourly and fixed-price

Chapter Two: All-Round Freelance Services

payments. The contest winner is also charged 10% of the project price or $5 (the higher value) once the contest handover is complete.

Just like Upwork, Freelancer can keep track of your work time by taking screenshots and logging your keystrokes via its desktop app. The invoice for milestone payment is generated every Monday and payment is released every Wednesday. You can take advantage of the platform's 'Dispute Resolution System' in case you have an issue with the transaction.

The available withdrawal methods are wire transfers to your bank (minimum amount of $500), PayPal, Freelancer debit card, and Skrill (does not support USD payments).

Receiving Feedback

Feedback is optional for both clients and freelancers. But if you are a freelancer, it is always better to ask your client to provide feedback so that you can position yourself higher than others when it comes to future projects. The feedback is accompanied by a rating system on a scale of 5. Completing several projects with high ratings would earn you a place in the 'Preferred Freelancer' program in which you can receive invitations to several exclusive, high-value projects and have an advantage on the search engine results.

Summary

All these platforms have proven to be highly useful to fetch work and help freelancers boost their full-time careers. If you are new to the freelancing world, we would highly recommend signing up for these three platforms and finding work there, at least until you build your portfolio.

No matter which platform you use, your duty as a freelancer is to submit high-quality work on time. Even though you are working from home, this job should be considered as any other professional job and taken seriously. If you excel in your work as a freelancer during your first few projects, you are highly likely to fetch more projects in the future.

Chapter Two: All-Round Freelance Services

The next three chapters will talk about particular freelancing skills that are very common and also in high demand. You will also learn more about the specific freelancing services that you should target—apart from the three we've already mentioned—to increase your chances of getting projects and earning more money.

Chapter Three: Programming and Graphic Design

Programming

The majority of programmers would like to work from the comfort of their meticulously configured home office, and thus, there is no shortage of talented freelancers in this segment. While most freelancing platforms on the Internet offer millions of job opportunities for this community, there are a few that specialize in this segment. Take a look at a brief overview of such platforms.

Toptal

Toptal is one of the most popular freelancing platforms for programmers and developers. The company claims that it only recruits the top 3% of freelancers in the world, thus making it a platform that many aspire to be on.

Signing Up

Unlike other freelancing platforms, becoming a

Chapter Three: Programming and Graphic Design

part of the Toptal community is not as simple as signing up and completing your profile. You have to apply for it like any other job and prove your mettle in coding through various stages of interviews to get on board. The first interview will include three questions and you'll need to answer at least two of them right to qualify for the next round, which will be carried out over Skype. The exclusive platform will open its doors to you if you clear the Skype interview.

Jobs and Projects

Toptal offers jobs and projects for software engineers who are aspiring to freelance on a full-time basis. Based on their skill sets, the programmers can develop projects related to Android, Java, and so many other categories. There are three types of engagement with clients: part-time, full-time, and hourly. You set up your profile, add skills and prep projects, fix your hourly rate, and start applying for relevant projects. An hourly rate of $50 to $85 is considered to be a decent starting point for new members.

You go through a client interview before being selected for a project. Each project has a trial period of two weeks. During this period, if the client is not satisfied with your work, they can cancel the contract and pay nothing to Toptal. However, the freelancer will be paid 50% of the expected income.

Scope and Method of Payment

While the detailed information about how much Toptal charges is not available, the website says that the average earning of its members is around $83,970, which should translate into $43 per hour. That is an impressive rate; but considering that the members are the best of the best, it is not surprising. The developers won't know the amount that the platform is charging its clients for the projects they have landed.

Invoices are generated every two weeks and it takes another two weeks for the payment to be completed. The payments can be transferred to

Chapter Three: Programming and Graphic Design

your local bank account, your PayPal account, or your credit, debit, or prepaid card.

Gigster

Just like TopTal, Gigster is a highly selective platform that has a comprehensive onboarding process. It claims to have the top 1% of talents in the tech industry and offers turnkey solutions to clients by assembling a team of freelancers to complete a big project under a project manager. Let's see how to become a Gigster.

Signing Up

Interested candidates can visit the website and fill in detailed information about the projects they have worked on in the past. Based on that, the company filters out applicants and the shortlisted ones will be subjected to a comprehensive interview with the top people who are already on the platform. The questions will primarily be technical to test the programmer's skills and depth of knowledge in his/her domain. They will also inspect the past code you have written. If they like what they see, your joining the network will be fast-tracked. Your first project will be considered a trial. There could also be a second interview before you enter the network.

Getting on a Project Team

Once you are in the network, Gigster will place you on a team to work on a client project with other developers. If things go well, you will be promoted to a full-time member of the network. The new freelancer will receive a 'karma amount' based on how well he/she performed in the interview. The karma points are an internal measure of the freelancer's reputation; a person with high karma points is usually one who has completed several projects with great results. The projects you are eligible to work on are also based on your karma points.

Payment

Gigster doesn't divulge detailed information about how it arrives at the pay scale for each indi-

Chapter Three: Programming and Graphic Design

vidual, but reveals that the hourly rate depends on the quality of work delivered. The company claims that it once paid a very talented iOS developer $650 per hour for his top-quality job! Either way, the platform says that the members will be paid as per San Francisco standards, irrespective of where they operate. A Reddit user who is also a Gigster says that on average, a freelancer earns about $5,000 per month.

In short, with its structural way of working in teams, Gigster tries to capture the best of both corporate and freelance worlds.

Gun.io

Gun.io is a direct rival to TopTal and Gigster. It brings freelance software developers together with business owners and entrepreneurs who seek their services. The platform focuses on onboarding highly skilled freelance programmers/software developers with vast experience.

Signing Up

Once you create a profile based on your skills and experience, the engineers go through as many as seven stages of assessment before letting you into the community of Gun.io. The assessment process involves a coding challenge, a Skype interview, a technical round, and finally, a character assessment with one of the top executives of the platform.

Getting Projects

When new projects come up, Gun.io handpicks candidates from its pool and introduces them to the client within 48 hours. Once you clear the three-stage vetting process and enter the pool of candidates that Gun.io calls the first circle, you are assigned a project to complete basic tasks. Once you complete them, you are assigned with more complicated tasks as a part of project-based interviewing.

Chapter Three: Programming and Graphic Design

Payment

The freelancers on Gun.io can determine their own hourly wages based on their skills and experience. According to the company, a client engagement (project) lasts 12 months on average, and is billed for around 1,000 hours. The platform has not furnished any statistics of the pay scale, but considering that only the elite and experienced can enter the community and that clients are ready to pay top dollar, expect the overall earnings to be up to par with Silicon Valley standards.

Graphic Design

As for graphic designers, they're usually creative souls that are wired to think differently. So, a corporate job or a conventional working arrangement is like chopping their wings off. This is exactly why they make excellent freelancers and there are a lot of online platforms that they could take advantage of to advance their careers. Let's look at a few.

99Designs

99Designs.com is one of the most popular freelancing platforms that focus on this niche. The website lists over 90 design categories and has a global community of freelance designers.

Signing Up

Signing up is free and simple. Once you are done with this step, you can start browsing for jobs directly. Needless to say, a comprehensive portfolio representing your range of skills and past work makes your profile appealing to clients.

Projects and Contests

The most popular aspect of 99Designs is its contests. The clients float a contest with a design brief and invite participants to submit their entries. Freelancers enter the contest if they find it suitable to their goals. The entry chosen by the client wins the prize money while the client retains the rights to their work. Usually, the winners go on to receive regular design projects from

Chapter Three: Programming and Graphic Design

the contest holder.

You can also respond to project invitations sent to you and work one-on-one with the client to collaborate and complete the design brief.

Payments

The contests usually offer over $200 of prize money and most contests can be completed in an hour or so. The payments are claimed to be processed within three business days. 99Designs charges the freelancers a sum of $100 to match them with clients and this money is recovered over the first $500 worth of charges from that client. In addition to that, there is also a platform fee that varies between 5% and 15%, depending on your skill level (top-level designers pay less).

The payments for the completed projects and contests won can be transferred to Payoneer (debit/credit card, direct transfer, global bank transfer) or PayPal.

Crowdspring

Crowdspring is a direct competitor to 99Designs and operates pretty much in the same way. The freelancing platform that specializes in designers claims to have over 200,000 registered creatives from across 195 countries.

Signing Up

Like every other sign-up process in the world, you use your email, create an account, and set up your password. Once you verify your contact details and upload your ID documents, you are asked to upload three samples of your previous work as a designer. Once all these items are verified by the Crowdspring team, you will be able to search for projects that suit you.

Projects and Contests

Just like 99Designs, Crowdspring primarily focuses on design contests and claims that each design contest created by clients receives an average of 100 entries. As a freelancer, you can browse the

Chapter Three: Programming and Graphic Design

contest posting, read the detailed brief, and submit your entry. If you get selected as the winner, you get paid. Alternatively, a client can also choose to invite a suitable designer for a one-on-one collaboration and decide on the price

Payment

After the completion of a project, the client fills out a survey that also includes rating the freelancer they worked with. A higher rating will enhance your chances of being invited to future projects. Payments are made within 14 days after the client's approval of the project through Payoneer or PayPal. The price of each project varies depending on its complexity and the effort involved. A simple logo design starts at $299 for the client.

Summary

These are the top freelance sites that you should target as a programmer or designer. Whether you are a graphic designer or a web designer, there is

Start Online Freelancing Today

something for everyone out there. If you're serious about pursuing this career, you should make the most of these dedicated websites today.

Chapter Four: Writing and Editing

You don't really need experience to become a freelance editor or a writer. But being an experienced writer or editor has its own perks. It helps you bring in a steady income and polish your skills.

As an experienced freelance writer, you can earn $50 for a 500-word article as a standard price. Ideally, the pay for any writing job depends on the quality, the level of your expertise, and the amount of work you can submit within a specific period. An inexperienced editor can charge around $20 an hour and an expert can charge up to $85 or more, depending on the task and client budget. Another important task within this niche is that of a proofreader. Once you are an acknowledged proofreader, you can charge up to $35 an hour.

Whether you are proficient in any of these skills or you are a newbie, you can find a legitimate website to work as a freelancer, where you can showcase your skills and get paid for the work you do.

Writing covers a broad category. There are jobs for writing news articles, books, Wikipedia entries, travel writing, job descriptions, product descriptions, etc. The list is huge and companies are looking for people in every language. Do not apply for a contract unless you are entirely fluent or, at the very least, conversant in the language required. A bad job may get paid, but a low rated review can torpedo your career before it is even started.

Copyscape

Before we look at the freelancing services, we should take a look at a service that many clients require of freelance writers. That is Copyscape.

Copyscape is a service that indexes copyrighted material and provides a search service to see if a piece of writing is plagiarizing existing content. The free service will take a look at indi-

Chapter Four: Writing and Editing

vidual webpages. The paid service allows you to check offline content, such as articles or books that are not yet published. They charge $0.03 for the first 200 words and $0.01 for every 100 words after. This means that a 1,000 word article will cost $0.83 to check for plagiarism and a 50,000 word novel will cost $5.02 to check. Many clients will insist on proof that this check has been done.

The list below suggests a few websites that hire freelancers based on various skill sets, but are highly reliable specifically for writers, editors, and proofreaders.

iWriter

For beginners who aspire to become a freelance writer, iWriter.com can be the best website to start with. There are different levels with different pay scales. Once you start receiving 5-star ratings for the content you produce, you can boost your profile. This will, in turn, help you earn extra money. And once you are an established content writer, you can get special requests from your clients, where you can keep 70% of the commission for the requested articles. You can choose the number of words you want to write per day, according to which you can take relevant orders after negotiating with the client.

Signing Up

Signing up on iWriter is simple. You start by registering yourself as a content writer for free and by providing personal information. While registering, you are prompted to write two articles of 200 words each. You can then request and choose jobs based on your preference. After connecting with the client, you can understand more about the project they are assigning. Avoid plagiarism and try to keep the quality high, as there are chances that your content might not be approved. Also, if you don't follow the requester's guidelines, your client will give you a poor rating. A bad rating and other factors can lead to a ban on your account. Once your article is approved, the payment will be made to your account. If the client

Chapter Four: Writing and Editing

doesn't approve your assignment within three days, the website will approve your content and the payment will be carried out.

Guru

This website offers numerous benefits, both for beginners and experts. Guru.com is dedicated to freelance writers where you can find ideal jobs based on your preference, by filtering your search. Guru.com offers various job opportunities within the sub-niche of writing and editing. You can work as a technical writer, blog writer, or copywriter, among many other titles. You can choose the job that is relevant to your skills and start getting projects in no time.

Signing Up

To sign up for Guru.com, you can register yourself for free or you can opt for a paid membership. The latter will give you additional incentives like quoting higher bids and paying a smaller amount of fees, depending on the type of membership you choose. If you want to downgrade your membership, you can just stop renewing it. However, once you sign up as a paid member, it is impossible to get a refund upon cancelation.

The registration process is fairly simple; you fill in your personal information and verify your email. Next, you create your profile by mentioning the services you will be offering. You then have to submit your ID for verification. Once you find a relevant assignment, you make your bid. You get to spend only a limited number of bids per month. Once you have exhausted your limit, you can buy more if you are still looking for more work. The payment will be made to your bank account or PayPal within two to three working days, once the work is finished and approved.

PeoplePerHour

This website allows you to connect with professionals on an hourly basis and also on the basis of relevant projects. Once you register with this website, you will be directed to the projects that

Chapter Four: Writing and Editing

match your skill set and profile. You can quote the price for your services according to your preference. After submitting the work to your client, they will rate your work. Your visibility in the search results will increase based on this. This way, you will become a certified freelancer on this site, after which you can offer your services to major clients and companies that are present on peopleperhour.com.

Signing Up

To sign up for PeoplePerHour, you need to complete an online form on the website. Next, you have to set up your profile, like any other normal freelance website. Once the application is reviewed and you meet all the requirements, you can start taking up projects. You can find jobs that are displayed by big businesses or independent entities, or you can make your own listings for a job and post them. Once you have submitted your work, you can write up an invoice, quote the price, and send it to the entity. Following this, the payment will be transferred to your account. The service will take a commission with every payment. The commision rates are based on how much you have billed each client. They are 20% for under $350, 7.5% between $350 and $7000, and 3.5% over $7000.

Constant Content

Constant-content.com hosts some big names such as eBay and Home Depot among its clients. Similar to other freelancing websites, you can arrange your workload according to your availability and schedule. You have the freedom of choosing whether you want to do a specific project individually or in a group. And like the other writing and editing websites, this website also frowns upon plagiarized content. You can choose jobs based on your expertise level.

Signing Up

The signing up process involves filling out basic details about yourself, after which you will be subjected to a short quiz. You will then be asked to submit a sample assignment of 100 to 250 words. Once your performance is deemed satisfactory, you can start taking up work that you might be interested in. Upon completion and submission of your assignment, your work will be reviewed. Client approval can take up to three to five business days. The payments on this site are made the first week of every month to your PayPal account.

Summary

As we've already pointed out, writing and editing are among the top skills that many companies and startups are looking for. If this seems to be the right path for you, start by signing up for any of these websites, then climb your way up after polishing your skills and gaining some valuable experience as a writer or editor.

Chapter Five: Marketing

As we've already mentioned in the first chapter, marketing ranks among the top in-demand skills. A lot of companies, both big and small, are looking for digital marketers that can help in promoting their brands and products. Since online traffic constantly keeps increasing, it is important to market every brand. In the past, it was easier to garner the attention of the general public, even without the help of a dedicated marketer. But with people heavily relying on websites, mobile applications, and e-commerce in general to get desired products and services, every company needs a digital marketer today.

As a digital marketer, you will be at a greater benefit if you possess various technical skills along with a creative mindset. Your chances of getting hired will increase even more if you have set an affordable price range.

Aside from Upwork and Fiverr (the details of which you already know), there are a few other

Chapter Five: Marketing

reliable freelancing platforms that you can use to get marketing projects. Ideally, these marketplaces or platforms will offer you the following benefits apart from helping you get projects:

- Build Your Network: Even though there is some competition, you can actually build your network by meeting several like-minded people and learning from them. If you are lucky, a few might help you by giving tips.
- Build Your Portfolio: Since these platforms ask for previous work due to client demand, you have to build your portfolio. Not only will it get you work but it will also help you stand out from the rest.
- Financial Aspects: Your payment will be processed securely, and you can easily know when your project will be rejected or asked to be revised.

Read on to find out about the best freelancing platforms for marketers and how to use each one of them to kick-start your marketing career.

ClearVoice

In order to be a part of this platform, you should submit a portfolio. Even though ClearVoice has a smaller talent pool than major websites like Fiverr, you will definitely get gigs through this platform after being vetted. Apart from digital marketers, ClearVoice also recruits designers, writers, and content strategists.

To begin working as a freelance marketer on ClearVoice, you should first complete your profile by building your CV portfolio. Once it is strong enough, you receive an invitation to become a part of the platform. To sign up, you need to access the 'For Freelancers' link on the main page. After filling in your name, click on 'Get Started.' You can then sign up using your email ID or Twitter account. After that, you need to build your CV and upload content for your sample work. Once you have developed your CV and portfolio, your account will be reviewed. If you manage to get in, you will be matched and presented with opportunities aligning with your skill set and pay rate.

Chapter Five: Marketing

Your clients can contact you through the in-app messaging service. For the payment method, you should know that ClearVoice cuts a 25% service fee for every accepted job. However, you will receive the exact amount you view on the gig. Your payments will be made through PayPal.

One important thing to note about ClearVoice is that you should not entirely rely on this platform to fetch projects. Instead, you can turn to it to build your network. It is extremely easy to set up your profile and get paid.

OnSite

OnSite is an exclusive freelancing platform that requires you to upload an online portfolio. It is then reviewed by a team that will decide whether you are eligible to join the OnSite community or not. Basically, this acts as a membership. You can also be invited by the team or by another member who is already enlisted. The official team takes quick decisions; you get to know within 24 hours whether your portfolio and request are approved or not. If you are lucky, instead of having to search for jobs, you'd be matched with clients upon their request—which will ultimately depend on your portfolio. Getting a freelance gig on On-Site solely depends on the client's decision. If they think you are unsuitable for a job, you are not allowed to make requests.

Apart from content and digital marketing, you also have the chance of being hired as an illustrator, developer, or designer. The platform has big names as clients, including Google, BBC, and Collins—no wonder they only hire 5% of freelancers that apply. To complete your profile, you have to enter your skills, experience, and hourly rate. The clients on this service expect top-quality work and timely submissions. They can browse through your work and 'save' you for further gigs. In this case, you will be notified when they try to approach you. So, it's safe to say that you just need a head start on this platform. Once you have it, your earning potential can majorly increase after a few years of experience. In fact, big compa-

Chapter Five: Marketing

nies will wait in line to hire you for projects. Another benefit of this site is that you can use it for free without having to pay for any bookings.

LinkedIn

Now, you might consider LinkedIn to be a source of full-time positions only. Not many people realize the potential of this social media platform for offering you freelance marketing jobs. In fact, LinkedIn has witnessed almost a 50% growth of freelancers over five years. With an enormous client base, you can search for multiple offers that are posted on the site on a daily basis.

You can sign up for LinkedIn using your email and build your professional profile. Be sure to add your profile picture; a professional-looking profile picture boosts your chances of getting approached. Another important aspect to focus on is your profile headline. Your clients will search for you based on your headline, which is why it is important to have one that is direct and descriptive. Speaking of this, you should also write your

'About' section after giving it enough thought. This will help the client understand your position, expertise, and experience. You should then upload your portfolio or add a link to your website. You can also upload your previous work—articles, media, posts, etc.—on the 'Featured' section. As a freelance digital marketer, you can showcase all the work you have done before to strengthen your profile.

Lastly, you should request endorsements from your connections, which can include your employers, supervisors, recruiters, and even colleagues. These are basically reviews that assess your skills. To get hired, you can either apply for freelance jobs on your main feed or connect with recruiters directly. Your payment method would be determined depending on the client.

Contently

Similar to other platforms, Contently also deals in hosting freelancers of varied skills but is highly preferred by marketers due to its success. To join

Chapter Five: Marketing

this community, you should upload a portfolio showing relevant work. You can then apply to the platform's talent network. It is, however, difficult to be accepted into the talent network because you need to be vetted. But if you are, you will have the opportunity of working with big brands such as Marriott, Google, IBM, and Walmart. After you get hired, your profile portfolio becomes visible to clients. You should beware of the ratings and punctuality in delivery.

How it works is that you get added to a content team if you are selected for it. You can then be hired by clients depending on your portfolio and minimum pay rate. Keep in mind that Contently hires some of the best professionals with diverse portfolios, which is why you would need to brush up on your skills and aim to build a high-quality portfolio. But if you are in, you can expect to be paid higher rates. The built-in messaging system is highly reliable and easy to use, which helps in keeping a tab on your conversations with clients. Another major benefit of entering this freelance platform is the opportunity to build a massive network with people whose work you'd appreciate and look up to. Also, you will have a reliable support team to assist you at every stage.

These sites are excellent platforms for you to get a head start on your career. You will be exposed to like-minded people, have great earning potential, and explore creative projects.

Conclusion

No matter which platform you use to find work as a freelancer, there are some common rules and guidelines to be followed. Freelancing is like any other paid work; you are expected to be honest about your profile, experience, and skill set. Similar to any nine-to-five job, you are expected to perform all tasks to the best of your ability and achieve high-quality results. No matter what service you offer, the end product, assignment, project, or work should be free of plagiarism and copyrighted materials.

It is not just about the quality of your work; effective communication, timely completion of tasks, and friendly manners are also the hallmark of a highly successful freelancer. While freelancing allows you to be flexible with your timings, it also requires discipline, commitment, and professional attitude to qualify as your full-time career path, depending on the nature of the job.

If you want to dodge the rush-hour commute,

be your own boss, sit in your pajamas, reserve the right to choose your projects, and still earn as much as your friend who is stuck in a corporate job, then it's time for you to make up your mind and jump into the world of freelancing. Assess your skills, sign up for a relevant website, and you'll have taken the first step toward working as a freelancer!

Online Resources

https://www.freelancer.com/community/articles/a-freelancer-s-guide-to-freelancer-com-introduction-to-freelancer-com

upwork.com

fiverr.com

http://99designs.com/

https://www.crowdspring.com/

https://www.iwriter.com/

https://www.peopleperhour.com/

https://www.peopleperhour.com/how-it-works

https://www.guru.com/

https://www.constant-content.com/freelance-writing-jobs.htm